Mind Your 'Ships'

Why One 'Ship' Won't Get You to Shore

How Mentors, Allies, Sponsors & Partners
Help You Get Noticed, Promoted & Paid
What You Deserve

Dr. Anesa Davis

Copyright © 2025 by Dr. Anesa Davis

All rights reserved. No part of this book may be reproduced in any form or by any electronic or mechanical means—including information storage and retrieval systems—without written permission from the author, except by a reviewer who may quote brief passages in a review.

Published by DMC Consulting Group
www.consultdmcgroup.com

Printed in the United States of America

First Edition: 2025

Cover design and interior layout by DMC Creative Team

ISBN: 979-8-9995386-1-1

Dedication

To my family – your love, support, and encouragement have been my anchor through every season. This book reflects the lessons, strength, and resilience I've gained because of you.

Acknowledgments

To my incredible friends – you saw my potential long before I did. Your encouragement, belief, and persistent nudging pushed me to share my knowledge in a way I never imagined. This book wouldn't exist without your voices reminding me that what I know matters.

Thank you for being my greatest allies and my strongest ships.

Foreword

Let me tell you upfront – this book is packed.

Not with fluff, but with real insight. It's going to challenge how you think about your career, your relationships, and maybe even your own expectations. Some of what you'll read may feel new. Some of it may feel obvious – but still uncomfortable. That's intentional.

I told a lot of people I was going to write a book that would show them *how* to build their ships – mentors, allies, sponsors, and partners. And I meant that. But here's the truth:

I can't give you *the* strategy.
Because there is no one-size-fits-all answer.

Your journey is yours – shaped by your goals, your environment, your identity, and your lived experiences. What works for me may not work exactly the same for you. And what moves one person forward might leave another stuck.

So instead of pretending there's a universal map, I've given you the compass.

Inside this book, you'll find the concepts, the mindset shifts, and the questions you need to start building – and maintaining – the relationships that matter most to your growth. But applying these ideas? That's where your story comes in. And if you're ready, I'm here to help you tailor it to your reality.

We'll talk more about that later.

For now, take a deep breath. Be open. Give yourself permission to reflect, wrestle, and take what you need from these pages. You don't have to absorb it all at once. You just have to begin.

Let's get into it.

Mind Your 'Ships'

Table of Contents

Introduction: One 'Ship' Won't Get You to Shore 11

Before We Begin: Let's Talk About Performance 17

Chapter 1: The Mentorship Mirage 21

Chapter 2: The Allyship Advantage 31

Chapter 3: The Sponsorship Shift 39

Chapter 4: The Partnership Principle 49

Chapter 5: Maintaining the Fleet 59

Chapter 6: Evolving Your Fleet for Long-Term Success 71

Closing: Don't Just Build It – Sail It 83

Bonus: "Ship Check" Self-Assessment 87

    Step 1: Rate Your Ships 87

    Step 2: Reflection Questions 88

    Step 3: Ship Goals 88

Reflection Recap 91

    Chapter 1: The Mentorship Mirage 91

    Chapter 2: The Allyship Advantage 92

    Chapter 3: The Sponsorship Shift 92

    Chapter 4: The Partnership Principle 93

    Chapter 5: Maintaining the Fleet 93

    Chapter 6: Evolving Your Fleet …Success 94

Next Steps / Stay Connected 97

    1. Put Your Reflection Into Action 97

2. Download Free Tools 98
  3. Book a Career Strategy Session 98
  4. Move Now – Don't Stop Here 98
  5. Let's Connect 99

About the Author 101

Resources 103

  Recommended Reads 103
  Career Tools 103
  Videos & Talks 103
  Templates & Downloads 104

Mind Your 'Ships'

Why One 'Ship' Won't Get You to Shore

How Mentors, Allies, Sponsors & Partners
Help You Get Noticed, Promoted & Paid
What You Deserve

Introduction: One 'Ship' Won't Get You to Shore

This book started with one unscripted moment.

I was giving a talk – no slides, just me sharing some hard-earned truths about career growth.

And out of nowhere, I said,
"Some of y'all are out here with 20+ mentors and don't have a single ally or sponsor on your team... some of y'all need to mind your ships."

The room. Went. Silent.
Then it erupted – laughter, lightbulbs, phones coming out.

People came up afterward quoting it back to me.
"Mind your ships – that's it. That's the whole message."

And honestly? They were right.

The phrase came to me because I'd seen so many smart, capable, talented people work themselves to the brink – only to stay stuck. Not because they lacked the skills. But because they didn't have the right relationships. They were floating through their careers in a single little boat, when what they needed was a whole fleet.

It hit me later why the line felt so familiar. It's a play on that sign you see at metro stations in London:

"Mind the gap."

It's a warning – a reminder to watch your step before you fall between where you are and where you're trying to go.

Mind your ships is the career version of that. Because for a lot of people, there's a gap between potential and opportunity – and the only thing that bridges it is the right relationships.

Now let me be clear – I'm not anti-mentor. Not even close.

Mentorship is valuable. But mentorship alone won't move you forward.

Especially not when the people mentoring you are just sharing advice and not advocating for you.

If your only ship is mentorship, you might float – but you won't go far.

You need a fleet.

You need:
- ✓ Allyship – the kind that shows up when it's inconvenient
- ✓ Partnership – the kind that builds with you, not just beside you
- ✓ Advocacy – the kind that multiplies your voice (bridge to sponsorship)
- ✓ Sponsorship – the kind that drops your name in rooms you didn't even know existed

And yes – you still need mentorship too.
But let's stop pretending it's the only ship that matters.

This book is for the person who's been working hard, doing all the "right" things, and still feels overlooked.
It's for the person who's tired of waiting for someone to notice, and ready to build relationships that make people notice.

Inside, we'll break down each type of ship – how to build it, what it looks like in real life, and how to avoid the common traps that keep people isolated or stuck.

You'll also get:
- Reflection prompts to apply it to your own career
- Real Talk moments (because you know I don't sugarcoat)
- And a simple framework to build your own strategic relationship "fleet"

This isn't a book about being more likable or adding people on LinkedIn.
It's about becoming the kind of professional people want to recommend, include, invite, and promote.

So go ahead – mind your ships.
Because one ship won't get you to shore.
But the right fleet?
It'll carry you all the way.

Before We Begin: Let's Talk About Performance

Before we dive into building your relationship "fleet," we need to level-set:

None of this works without performance.

It may not be the most exciting topic, but it's the foundation.
All the allyship, mentorship, and sponsorship in the world won't move your career forward if your work doesn't speak for itself.

Relationships can open doors.
Performance is what earns you the right to stay in the room – and be trusted in it.

Let's be clear:
This isn't about "who you know" replacing "what you do."
It's about combining results and relationships to unlock momentum.

Because you've seen it – we all have:

- Someone who's well-connected but not reliable
- A person who talks a big game but can't back it up
- An opportunity handed to someone... who fumbles it in plain sight

That's not elevation. That's exposure.

So here's the expectation:

If you're reading this, I believe you're someone who cares about doing the work – not just showing up, but showing up prepared, accountable, and committed to growth.

This book is about making sure your performance gets the visibility and support it deserves.

You don't have to be perfect. But you do need to be excellent at the essentials:

- ✓ Follow through
- ✓ Deliver results
- ✓ Own your development

✓ Bring a standard of excellence to everything you do

Do that consistently – and the right relationships will help you amplify it.

Let's get started.

Chapter 1: The Mentorship Mirage

Let's kick this off with a little honesty: Mentorship is the most overused, oversold, and under-leveraged relationship in most people's careers.

That's not shade – it's the truth. Somewhere along the way, we turned mentorship into this mythical career-saving lifeline. Everyone says you need a mentor. College programs pair you with one. Conferences tell you to find one. Some folks even brag about having a whole board of mentors like it's LinkedIn Pokémon.

But here's the problem: mentorship alone won't move you. At least not far.

I can't count how many people I've coached who told me, "I don't get it. I have mentors. I've done everything they said. I'm working hard. Why am I still stuck?"

And I have to break it to them – gently, but directly:
You've got advice. But do you have access?

You've got guidance. But do you have visibility?

You've got encouragement. But do you have elevation?

See, that's the mentorship mirage – it looks like progress, but it's often just more walking in circles.

Let me say this louder: Mentors are not always movers.

What Mentorship Is Good For

Let me be clear – I'm not anti-mentor. Mentorship has value. At its best, a mentor offers:

- Perspective from lived experience
- Honest feedback (when they're brave enough to give it)
- A sense of support – "you're not alone in this"
- Guidance for the road you're on

Those things are not small. But they're also not enough.

A mentor can help you sharpen your skills, improve your mindset, or navigate a tough moment. But if they're not connected to the power levers in your organization – if they don't actively advocate for you – their advice becomes just that: advice. Not opportunity.

And here's where people get stuck.

They collect mentors the way others collect quotes on Pinterest – cute, inspiring, and completely disconnected from the action they need to take.

What Mentorship Won't Do (By Itself)

Mentors don't get you promoted.

Mentors don't drop your name in executive meetings.

Mentors don't always have the power – or the will – to take risks on your behalf.

I've seen people mentored for years without being seen as promotable. Why? Because mentorship is often passive. It's advice at lunch. It's check-ins every quarter. It's, "Have you thought about taking a class on that?"

Meanwhile, someone else – with less experience but more access – gets the opportunity. Not because they're better, but because someone actively positioned them.

Let that sink in.

Let's be real – mentorship is often private praise with no public impact.
They'll compliment your ideas one-on-one, but in meetings? Crickets.

That disconnect is where careers stall. You don't just need someone who believes in you. You need someone who bets on you.

The Relationship Trap

Here's a tough truth: some mentors love mentoring because it keeps them in control.

They can share knowledge without risk. They get the warm fuzzy of being helpful without putting anything on the line. And if you don't succeed? They sleep fine.

But a real career-moving relationship requires risk. Visibility. Stretch.

If your mentor isn't willing to go beyond coffee chats and articles to read – if they're not

creating pathways or challenging your comfort zone – you've got a cheerleader, not a career lifter.

Are You Hiding in Mentorship?

Here's a question I ask in coaching sessions: Are you using mentorship as a strategy – or a shield?

Sometimes, we stay in the mentorship loop because it's safe. You don't have to ask for anything big. You don't have to be vulnerable. You get to stay in the land of "maybe later" instead of "move now."

But staying in constant learning mode without execution is just procrastination in a business suit.

At some point, you've got to move from mentee to momentum.

That starts by building the right relationships – the ones we'll cover in the chapters ahead.

Red Flags: When Mentorship Isn't Helping

- ✓ They never bring up your name when you're not in the room
- ✓ You've been in the same role for years, but they keep saying "just wait"
- ✓ They offer safe advice but never challenge your thinking
- ✓ You leave conversations inspired but without any real next steps
- ✓ They avoid connecting you to their network or pulling you into opportunities

If you see those signs, it's time to reassess. Not cut off – but recalibrate.

You can still appreciate them. You can still learn from them. But you don't have to stay stuck thinking that mentorship is the final destination. It's just the launchpad.

Reflection Prompts

- Who are my current mentors – and what value do they actually provide?
- Do I rely too heavily on mentorship to avoid taking bolder action?
- Have I ever mistaken encouragement for elevation?
- When's the last time someone vouched for me without me being in the room?
- What would change if I focused more on sponsors, allies, and advocates?

Real Talk

If you've got a mentor who's been "mentoring" you for years, but you're still in the same place – that's not mentorship. That's career stagnation with a friendly face.

The mentorship model isn't broken. It's just incomplete.
Mentorship is the warm-up. Not the win.
It's preparation – not propulsion.

The good news?
You're not stuck. You're just floating in the wrong ship.

And now, it's time to build your fleet.

Quick Check: Are You Collecting or Connecting?

- ✓ Are you "collecting" mentors like trophies, but still feeling unseen?
- ✓ Do you have 10+ mentors – but no sponsor, ally, or advocate?

- ✓ Are you having career convos that sound inspiring but go nowhere?

If so, it's time to trade quantity for quality – and start building relationships that create motion, not just mentorship.

Chapter 2: The Allyship Advantage

Let's start with a moment we've all experienced.

You speak up in a meeting, say something insightful... and it's ignored. Ten minutes later, someone else says the same thing – suddenly it's genius.

Or maybe you're up for a stretch assignment, but no one advocates for you when decisions are made. You're capable. Qualified. But invisible.

Now imagine this:

What if someone had said, "Actually, I'd like to circle back – I think what she said earlier was exactly the right direction."

What if someone in that room dropped your name – not because you were there, but because you deserved to be.

That's allyship in motion.

And the truth is: most careers don't need more effort – they need more allies.

What Allyship Really Is

Allyship gets tossed around a lot, especially in corporate diversity statements. But true allyship isn't performative – it's proactive.

At its core, allyship means:

- Seeing someone's value – even when others don't
- Using your influence to amplify their presence, voice, or opportunity
- Standing up, speaking up, and showing up when it actually matters

This is not about being nice. It's about being intentional.

A real ally doesn't just "support" you in theory.
They position you.

They repeat your ideas when others try to claim them. They back you when the room gets quiet. They correct the record when credit goes to the wrong person.

And they do it whether or not you see it happen.

The Power of Allyship in Action

Let me tell you a story.

A colleague once told me about a time early in her career when she led a major project – designed it, managed it, delivered it. But when the executive debrief came, her manager presented the results like he was the lead.

She didn't have the title or confidence to speak up – but someone else did. A teammate jumped in and said, "Just to clarify, that project was actually led by [her name] – she deserves the credit."

That moment changed everything for her. Leadership took notice. Her credibility skyrocketed. She ended up promoted six months later.

That's what allyship looks like.
It's not about grand gestures.
It's about small moments that shift outcomes.

Allyship ≠ Friendship

Let's make a clear distinction here: an ally is not just a friend at work.

Your work BFF might grab coffee with you and vent about your boss – but an ally asks how they can help you be seen and heard.

Your friend might say "you got this."
An ally says, "I talked to the director and mentioned your name for that role."

You don't have to be besties to be allies.
You just need alignment – shared values, mutual respect, and a willingness to show up for each other when it counts.

How to Spot an Ally (Or Become One)

Signs someone's an ally:

- ✓ They give you credit when others forget to
- ✓ They make room for you to speak
- ✓ They advocate for your ideas without being asked
- ✓ They share their platform – not just their opinion

Ways to become one:

- o Pay attention to whose voice gets overlooked, then lift it
- o Interrupt interruptions (yes, that's a real thing)
- o Speak names in rooms where decisions get made
- o Don't wait to be asked – offer the recommendation

And here's the kicker – allyship is a two-way street.

You don't have to "wait" for someone to become your ally. Start being one, and you'll often find those relationships reciprocated and reinforced over time.

The Allyship Gap

Here's something no one tells you: many people think they're allies... but they're not.

They're nice colleagues.

They say "you did great" after the meeting – but stay silent when it counts.
They send encouragement in DMs – but never speak your name in public.

Intent without action is not allyship.
Allyship requires risk.

Because here's the truth: if it's always comfortable, it's not allyship – it's convenience.

Reflection Prompts

- Who has acted as an ally for me in the past – and how did it change my outcome?
- Am I showing up for others in meaningful, proactive ways – or just being supportive from the sidelines?
- When was the last time I spoke up for someone else who was being overlooked?
- Are my allies in the right rooms – or do I need to build new relationships to expand my support system?
- What's one way I can be more intentional in how I advocate for others?

Real Talk

You don't need 100 people hyping you in the breakroom.
You need 1–2 people who will speak your name when you're not in the room.

Allyship is the amplifier. It takes what you're already doing – and makes sure the right people hear it, see it, and respect it.

You're not asking for favors.
You're building bridges – ones that go both ways.

And when it's time to walk into the next level of your career, you won't have to walk alone.

Chapter 3: The Sponsorship Shift

Let's get into the ship that actually moves you: sponsorship.

If mentorship is about guidance, and allyship is about amplification, then sponsorship is about elevation.

Sponsorship is the difference between someone saying,
"I believe in your potential"
and someone saying,
"I'm putting my name and reputation behind you – let's go."

Let's break this down.

What Sponsorship Really Means

Sponsorship isn't just support – it's investment.

A sponsor is someone with influence, visibility, and decision-making power who actively advocates for your advancement. They're the person who brings your name into a room full of closed doors – and keeps saying it until one opens.

Sponsors don't just vouch for your work.
They create opportunity.
They position you for visibility.
They push your name forward in rooms you haven't entered yet.

And here's the key: they do it with intention.

They're not guessing. They've seen your results, they trust your capability – and they're willing to spend their own capital (reputational or otherwise) to get you where you need to go.

Sponsorship Requires Risk

This is what separates sponsors from mentors.

A mentor gives advice. A sponsor takes action.

A mentor might say, "You're doing great – keep it up."
A sponsor says, "I recommended you for the next-level role. Start preparing."

That's risk. That's boldness. That's career-shifting courage.

And that's why not everyone can be – or will be – a sponsor.

Not Everyone Deserves a Sponsor

Let's tell the whole truth: sponsorship is earned.

You can't network your way into someone vouching for you if you haven't done the work. Sponsors are high-stakes players – they have something to lose. They're not going to bet on potential alone. They bet on performance, readiness, and trust.

They have to believe:

o You'll deliver when it counts

- You'll represent them well
- You're ready for what they're opening up to you

If they're putting your name on the table, it has to be because they believe you'll elevate the room you're walking into – not drain its credibility.

So, how do you earn sponsorship?
By making your performance undeniable.
By showing up consistently with results, professionalism, and resilience.
By staying ready so no opportunity catches you off guard.

The Advocacy Bridge

Before someone becomes your sponsor, they often start as an advocate.

An advocate is someone who speaks positively about you – even if they don't have the authority to move the needle themselves.

They're the ones who say:
"You should talk to her – she really knows her stuff."
"He handled that project flawlessly – keep an eye on him."

Advocacy is public support. It's not always high-stakes, but it's strategic.

And here's the secret: many sponsors start as advocates who keep watching.

If you're earning consistent, visible praise from people around you, don't ignore that. Cultivate it. Relationships built on authentic respect often lead to deeper professional alignment.

Your next sponsor may be the colleague or manager who starts by simply advocating for your name in the right spaces.

How to Attract Sponsors (Without Being Awkward)

You can't demand a sponsor – but you can position for one.

Here's how:

Be excellent consistently. Sponsors watch before they act. Be visible in how you contribute, lead, and influence.

Deliver beyond your role. If you only do what's on your job description, you're easy to overlook. Add value across teams, solve problems, and show leadership in action.

Be bold about your goals. Sponsors don't guess. They need to know what you're aiming for – so they know when and where to lift you.

Build trust. Be someone whose name they can speak without hesitation.

Say thank you – and stay ready. If someone advocates for you, acknowledge it and deliver beyond expectations.

The Problem With "Invisible" Talent

Here's where a lot of high-performing professionals get stuck:

They do great work quietly.
They assume their results will speak for themselves.
They believe merit will be enough.

But in today's world, visibility matters just as much as capability.

If decision-makers don't know you – they can't sponsor you.

This doesn't mean you have to be flashy. But it does mean you need to be seen. Your ideas, your work ethic, your leadership – it all has to have a spotlight, not just a file folder.

Reflection Prompts

o Who are the people in my organization who have influence and visibility?

- Have I positioned myself as someone they can trust and elevate?
- What opportunities have I missed because no one was speaking my name?
- Am I focused only on doing the work – or also on being seen doing it?
- What would it look like to prepare for sponsorship instead of waiting for it?

Real Talk

Mentors will encourage you.
Allies will affirm you.
But sponsors? Sponsors will move you.

They are the ones who shift the room when you're not even in it.

And the biggest career breakthrough you've been waiting on?

It might not come from more hard work.
It might come from the right person saying your name at the right moment.

That's not politics. That's positioning.

It's not about playing the game.
It's about understanding the field – and making sure you're not sitting on the bench while opportunities pass you by.

Sponsorship is the real power ship.
So stop trying to sail your career solo.

It's time to let someone else help you accelerate.

Chapter 4: The Partnership Principle

Let's talk about the ship that too many people sleep on – partnership.

When you think about moving forward in your career, you probably think about finding people who can help you. But there's another layer – people you can build with.

That's what partnership is all about.

While mentorship, allyship, and sponsorship tend to flow vertically (someone ahead pulling you up), partnership is horizontal. These are your peers, your collaborators, your growth-mates. The people who are building at the same time you are – and pushing you as they climb too.

These relationships don't just fuel your goals – they sharpen them.

Partnership = Mutual Growth

A true partnership is rooted in reciprocity.

It's not just, "You help me and I'll help you someday."
It's, "We're both going somewhere – and we're better together."

Think of:

- That colleague who checks in after a tough meeting and shares how they'd handle it
- A peer who pushes you to apply for a role you wouldn't have gone after on your own
- A friend in another industry who shares insights that expand how you lead

They're not your boss. They're not your mentor. They're your partner – in growth, in goals, in mindset.

And here's the kicker: great partnerships often become lifelong career assets.

Partnerships Keep You Sharp

When you're surrounded by people who challenge you to do better, think deeper, and show up stronger – you grow faster.

They don't just cheer you on.
They push you.
They question you.
They expect excellence from you.

And because the relationship is mutual, you do the same for them.

This is how top performers stay sharp – they stay surrounded.

You need voices around you that won't let you shrink, coast, or stay stuck.

How to Build Strategic Partnerships

Let's get tactical. Strategic partnerships don't happen by accident. You have to be intentional.

Here's how to cultivate them:

Look sideways, not just up. Scan your peer group. Who's doing excellent work? Who's thinking differently? Who challenges the norm with substance?

Offer value first. Don't ask for coffee just to "pick their brain." Come in with perspective, encouragement, or insight. Real partnership begins with mutual respect.

Stay consistent. Relationships fade when you only check in when you need something. Build rhythm. Share resources. Stay visible.

Collaborate when possible. Whether it's co-presenting, brainstorming, or simply holding each other accountable – create real interaction.

Celebrate and elevate. A win for your partner is a win for the whole fleet. Share their wins publicly. Pass the mic. Make it known you rise together.

Partnership vs. Performance Competition

One of the biggest killers of partnership is the scarcity mindset.

The belief that there's only room for one of you to shine.
That if someone else is winning, your chances are shrinking.

But that's not how long-term success works.

You don't lose by clapping for someone else.
You don't fall behind by collaborating.
You win when you build circles where everyone's growth is supported.

Iron sharpens iron. And insecure people dull everyone's shine.

Reflection Prompts

- Who are three peers I respect and could grow with?
- Do I reach out consistently, or only when I need something?

- How can I become a stronger partner to others in my network?
- Have I unintentionally competed with someone I could have collaborated with?
- What's one intentional action I can take to strengthen a peer relationship this month?

Real Talk

You don't need a room full of executives to grow.
Sometimes you just need one peer who gets it – and who won't let you settle.

Partnership isn't just a support system. It's a growth accelerator.

Because when you build with the right people?
You don't just survive the storm – you build bigger ships together.

Let's not just climb the ladder.
Let's build bridges as we go.

Real Partnership in Action

Let me tell you about two women – one in finance, one in healthcare – who met during a leadership program I led a few years back. They had never crossed paths before, but on day one, they locked into each other's energy. They weren't competing. They were building.

After the program, they kept in touch. They started trading ideas. One would send an article and the other would send a podcast. Then came the real growth – co-hosting panels, giving each other feedback on stretch assignments, helping one another prep for performance reviews.

Fast forward three years: both are now in executive roles. Each has been promoted. Each has been publicly endorsed by the other. And when I asked one of them what made the

biggest difference in her trajectory, she said: "I had someone who wasn't afraid to call me higher – and remind me who I was when I forgot."

That's partnership. No titles required. Just mutual belief and consistent action.

Mistakes That Sabotage Partnerships

Not every connection turns into a strong partnership – and some fail because of unspoken missteps.

Here are a few to watch out for:

Being transactional. If your only engagement is asking for help or support, it's not partnership – it's extraction.

Inconsistency. Relationships need rhythm. Don't go ghost for a year and then pop back up asking for favors.

Competitiveness. You can't truly partner with someone you're secretly trying to outperform.

Over-relying on one person. Don't make someone your only sounding board. Diversify your partnerships and protect their capacity.

Lack of follow-through. If someone gives you insight, connection, or advice – use it. Show that their investment mattered.

The Scarcity Trap

Let's stay with this for a moment.

Scarcity says, "If they shine, I disappear." Partnership says, "If they shine, it lights up the path for me too."

Scarcity is what makes people hoard information. It's why folks stay silent when they see opportunities. It's the root of performative friendships – where the relationship only works as long as one person stays "on top."

But healthy partnerships kill scarcity.

They build confidence that we're not just running solo races – we're in a relay. Sometimes you're passing the baton. Sometimes you're running anchor. But you're always moving – together.

There's no limit on success. But there is a limit on how long you can win alone.

Extend the Circle

If you already have great partners – amazing. But don't stop there.

Reach back.
Reach across.
Invite someone in.

Because someone out there is craving connection, direction, and a bit of push – just like you were.

Be the person who builds the bridge. You just might build your own breakthrough in the process.

Chapter 5: Maintaining the Fleet

Let's be honest – it's one thing to build relationships. It's another thing to maintain them.

We all start out with good intentions.
"Let's stay in touch!"
"We should collaborate soon!"
"I'll check in next quarter!"

And then... life.

Work gets busy. Projects pile up. The calendar overflows. And before you know it, those valuable ships you've built? They're just names collecting dust in your contacts.

That's not a strategy – that's drift.

If you want a network that actually works, you have to maintain your fleet.

Relationships Are Like Plants

Stay with me.

Relationships don't need daily attention, but they do need intentional care.

- Mentorship can wither if you never update them on your progress.
- Allyship fades if you stop engaging in shared spaces.
- Sponsorship dies quietly if your performance slips and you fall off the radar.
- Partnership stalls when there's no rhythm or collaboration.

People forget who you are when you disappear – or worse, they remember you only as who you used to be.

Maintaining relationships doesn't have to be exhausting. But it does have to be intentional.

Easy Ways to Keep Your Ships Afloat

You don't need to send weekly updates or force awkward check-ins.

Here are some simple ways to stay visible and valuable:

Send quick wins: Share an article, congratulate a promotion, forward a podcast. No ask. Just value.

Add check-ins to your calendar: Pick one contact each week to reconnect with. Fifteen minutes goes a long way.

Keep them in the loop: If someone helped you land a role or push through a tough season – tell them. Let them know their investment paid off.

Use milestones: Promotions, birthdays, work anniversaries – built-in reasons to reach out authentically.

Be helpful, not transactional: Don't wait until you need something. Add value first and often.

What If the Ship Has Drifted?

It happens.

Maybe you dropped the ball. Maybe they did. Maybe life just got in the way.

It's okay.

Here's your play:

Acknowledge the gap. "I've been meaning to reach out – it's been a minute!"

Show appreciation. "I still remember what you said about [X] – that stuck with me."

Re-establish the connection. "I'd love to reconnect and hear what you've been up to."

People are more gracious than we assume – especially when you lead with authenticity and respect.

Let Some Ships Sail

Now this part is important.

Not every relationship needs to last forever. Some ships serve their season – and that's okay.

- That mentor who helped you get your first promotion? Maybe you've outgrown the guidance.
- That peer you used to bounce ideas off of? Maybe they've shifted directions.
- That ally who had your back? Maybe their values no longer align with yours.

Releasing a ship doesn't mean there's conflict. It means you're making space for new alignment. Don't cling to connections that no longer support your momentum.

Make room. Stay grateful. Move forward.

A Note on Boundaries

You can't maintain your fleet if you're constantly overextending.

Be intentional, not available to everyone at all times. Relationships are powerful, but they shouldn't drain you.

- Set expectations clearly.
- Be honest about your capacity.
- Don't feel guilty about seasons of quiet – just circle back when you can.
- Protect your peace and your calendar.

You need fuel to steer your own ship, too.

Reflection Prompts

- Who in my network have I unintentionally drifted from?
- What small habits can I build to stay more connected?
- Are there any ships I'm forcing that I need to release?
- Have I been so focused on building that I've forgotten to maintain?
- What relationships have sustained me – and how can I honor them?

Real Talk

This isn't just about career strategy – it's about stewardship.

Because if you're only building relationships to get ahead, you'll always be chasing. But when you build them to grow together, you create something lasting.

You're not collecting ships. You're cultivating a fleet.

And if you've made it this far, you're not just learning how to move – you're learning how to lead.

So keep showing up.
Keep investing.
Keep minding your ships.

Because the right fleet can carry you farther than you ever could've sailed alone.

More Than a Check-In: A Story of Return

Let me share a quick story. A few years back, I worked with a brilliant analyst – sharp, resourceful, and on the rise. We kept in touch here and there, mostly around project cycles. Then one day, she reached out to me out of the blue.

"I think I messed up," she said.

Turns out, she'd gone silent on several mentors and collaborators during a demanding job transition. No updates. No thank-you's. Just vanished. She was afraid to reach out and "look ungrateful."

But guess what? When she finally did – when she took a moment to share where she was, how their input helped her land a major role, and how much she valued their past support – they welcomed her back with open arms.

One mentor even said, "I knew you'd be back. I just hoped you'd remember the door was always open."

Moral of the story: if the relationship had value, a genuine return *restores* trust – it doesn't destroy it.

Don't let embarrassment rob you of reconnection.

The Burnout Trap: When You Try to Maintain Too Much

Let's talk boundaries – for real.

One reason people stop maintaining their fleet is simple: they try to do too much for too many.

At some point, your inbox turns into a to-do list for other people's needs. Every lunch becomes a pitch meeting. Every call turns into a mini coaching session.

You weren't trying to be a martyr – just a good person.

But now you're tired. You're drained. And you're low-key resenting people you once loved supporting.

This is your sign: cut back to move forward.

Here's what helps:

Pick your priority people. Not everyone is "core fleet." Choose 5–10 key ships to pour into consistently.

Create a rotation. Monthly check-ins? Quarterly updates? Whatever works – just be realistic.

Set boundaries with clarity. "Hey, I'd love to connect, but I'm booked until next month." Short. Direct. Respectful.

Say no without guilt. Protecting your peace is productive.

Maintenance is about quality, not quantity.

A Visual Guide: Ship Maintenance Checklist

Use this once a quarter to stay on track:

- ✓ Have I updated key mentors/sponsors on major progress?
- ✓ Have I celebrated a win with my peer partners?
- ✓ Have I checked in with an ally who supported me recently?
- ✓ Have I removed or released relationships that no longer align?
- ✓ Have I offered value without being asked?

Print it. Post it. Practice it.

Maintaining your fleet takes less effort than rebuilding from scratch – but only if you stay consistent.

Chapter 6: Evolving Your Fleet for Long-Term Success

Building a fleet is one thing. Steering it into the future – that's another level.

Career seasons change. Industries shift. People move on. What served you well last year might need a serious upgrade next year. And the relationships that helped you get your first promotion might not be the ones to get you to the executive table.

This chapter is about evolution – not just maintenance. Because you weren't meant to stay in the same place, and neither were your ships.

The Relationship Lifecycle

Just like roles and responsibilities change, so do relationships.

Here's a helpful way to think about the natural lifecycle of a career ship:

Discovery – You meet. There's value, energy, curiosity.

Momentum – You're learning, connecting, growing together.

Stabilization – The rhythm forms. You trust each other.

Drift or Deepen – The relationship either fades or evolves.

Renewal or Release – You decide to reinvest... or let it go.

Recognizing where a relationship stands helps you avoid two traps:

- Over-loyalty to outdated dynamics
- Under-investment in new opportunities

Don't cling to a ship that no longer sails – and don't forget to upgrade your fleet as you level up.

Making Room for New Ships

You can't hold onto every relationship forever. And honestly, you shouldn't.

The higher you go, the more strategic your relationships must become. That doesn't mean cutting people off. It means curating your energy and investing it where there's mutual alignment and growth.

Ask yourself:

- Who challenges me to think differently?
- Who's already where I want to be?
- Who sees potential in me that I haven't fully owned yet?

These are the ships you want to invest in.

And here's a little secret: most people don't evolve their network. They keep recycling the same advice, same mindset, and same limited opportunities – then wonder why nothing's changing.

If you want transformation, your relationships must transform too.

Don't Forget to Level Up with People

While you're looking up the ladder, don't forget to look beside you. Some of the most powerful relationships you'll ever build are with people who grow with you – not just those already ahead of you.

- The peer who becomes a partner.
- The junior employee who becomes a founder.
- The mentee who ends up teaching you something major.

Investing in growth-minded people today builds your leadership circle for tomorrow. Because when you evolve together – that's legacy.

Signs a Relationship Needs to Evolve

- ✓ You only talk about the past.
- ✓ You feel drained after every conversation.
- ✓ They see you as who you were, not who you're becoming.

- ✓ The dynamic feels performative, not authentic.
- ✓ You're afraid to set boundaries.

These aren't signs of failure – they're signs it's time for a shift. Some ships need a new map. Others need a new captain. And some just need a thank-you and release.

Be honest about what's working – and what isn't.

Keep Stretching

Here's the hard truth: if you're the most ambitious person in your fleet, you need a new fleet.

You should be in rooms where:

1. You're not the smartest person there.
2. You're a little nervous (but excited) to speak up.
3. You leave with more questions than answers.

4. Your assumptions get challenged – not coddled.

That kind of discomfort? It's a gift. It keeps your growth muscles flexed.

You need relationships that stretch your strategy, your confidence, your vision. Because ships that stay in shallow waters never reach new shores.

Reflection Prompts

- What relationships helped me get to this stage of my career?
- Which ones are still aligned with where I'm headed?
- Where do I need to deepen – or release – a connection?
- Who do I admire but haven't reached out to yet?
- What's one way I can evolve my network over the next 90 days?

Real Talk

Growth requires grief. That's what no one tells you.

Sometimes evolving means letting go of people you love. Or stepping away from roles you once fought for. Or accepting that not everyone will come with you.

That's okay.

You don't owe anyone stagnation just to prove you're loyal.

You owe yourself growth. You owe your future the chance to become what it's supposed to be.

So as you evolve – so should your fleet.

Some ships will stay. Some will go. But as long as you keep sailing with intention, there will always be new waters to explore – and the right fleet to get you there.

Evolving Together: A Story from the Field

Let me tell you about Marcus.

When I met Marcus, he was a mid-level manager at a regional firm. He had a strong fleet – loyal mentors, supportive peers, and a few budding mentees. He credited his early success to the relationships he'd nurtured, and rightly so.

But over time, Marcus noticed something odd. While his career was progressing, his circle stayed the same. His conversations began to feel repetitive. His mentors were giving outdated advice. His peers were comfortable – not hungry. And the few people challenging him? He was avoiding them because they made him uncomfortable.

One day, during a leadership retreat, someone asked, "Who's helping you grow *now*?"

That hit hard.

Marcus realized his relationships weren't wrong – they were just rooted in a past version of himself. It wasn't disloyal to evolve beyond them. It was necessary.

So he did three things:

1. Reached out to two leaders in industries he admired – and asked to learn.
2. Joined a mastermind group with people outside his comfort zone.
3. Had honest conversations with old mentors, expressing appreciation and gently shifting the dynamic.

Six months later, Marcus was thinking bigger, stretching further, and playing at a level his old circle couldn't have prepared him for.

Evolving his fleet didn't mean forgetting his past – it meant building a future.

Upgrade Your Fleet: New Ships, New Capabilities

Think of your fleet like a growing organization. At first, you only need a few core roles. But as your journey expands, so must your fleet.

Ask yourself:

- Do I have a ***visionary sponsor*** who sees what I can't yet?
- Do I have a ***connector*** who opens doors I wouldn't find on my own?
- Do I have a ***strategist*** who helps me think longer term?
- Do I have an ***accountability partner*** who holds the mirror up when needed?

Each of these relationships serves a function – and you need to audit your fleet regularly.

Are you covered? Are there gaps? Are you carrying "dead weight" out of guilt or routine?

Don't be afraid to recruit new energy into your network.

Just like a company brings in new talent to meet the moment – so should you.

Common Mistakes That Block Growth

Let's be real. Most people stall not because of lack of talent – but because of relationship inertia.

Here are a few traps to avoid:

Loyalty over alignment: Staying tied to relationships that no longer fit your values or goals.

Familiarity bias: Only listening to the same voices you've always trusted.

Avoiding stretch conversations: Dodging people who challenge your thinking.

Under-networking: Waiting too long to build new connections until you "need" them.

Growth favors the proactive – not the passive.

A Visual Reminder: You're the Captain

As your career evolves, so should your role in steering the fleet.

You're not just a passenger anymore – you're the captain. That means you:

- ✓ Chart the course.
- ✓ Decide who's on board.
- ✓ Communicate direction.
- ✓ Maintain alignment.

Captains who cling to old maps crash in new waters. So update your charts, check your fleet, and move forward with clarity.

Closing: Don't Just Build It – Sail It

You've mapped out the ships that matter – mentors, allies, sponsors, partners, and the evolving fleet you'll need along the way.

You've reflected. You've questioned. You've seen yourself in a few of these pages (and probably side-eyed a few former colleagues too – it's okay, I did too).

Now here's where the book ends – but your movement begins.

Because knowing what ships you need means nothing if you don't use them.

This is not a theory to memorize. It's a fleet to build. A set of sails to raise. A route to chart that doesn't just lead to a title or a salary increase – but to something better:

Career clarity. Access. Confidence. Influence. Purpose.

Whatever your goal – the next promotion, a pivot into leadership, building your personal brand, or simply not feeling invisible in a sea of coworkers – the fleet helps get you there.

But only if you steer.

So let's leave you with this:

Real Talk – One Last Time

If you're waiting for someone to notice you, pick you, or promote you because you "did everything right"... you'll be waiting a long time.

Ships don't build themselves.

Doors don't open just because you stand in front of them looking prepared.

And careers don't grow in isolation – they grow in community, in conversation, and in bold, intentional action.

That starts with you.

Start that conversation.
Ask for the sponsorship.
Be a better partner.
Reconnect with that ally.
Audit your fleet and evolve.

You don't have to be perfect. You just have to move.
Because motion builds momentum.

And momentum? That's what gets you to shore.

One Last Prompt:

Before you close this book, write down:

1. One person you need to reconnect with
2. One ship you're ready to build (and how you'll start)
3. One ship you're finally ready to release

Then give yourself a deadline. Put it on your calendar. Don't wait for the "perfect" time – do it scared, but do it now.

Bonus: "Ship Check" Self-Assessment

A quick audit to see if your fleet is built to sail:

Whether you're early in your career or sitting in the C-suite, this check-in can reveal where you're strong, where you're coasting, and where you've got work to do. Be honest. This isn't about judgment – it's about clarity.

Step 1: Rate Your Ships

For each of the following ships, rate your current situation from 1 (nonexistent) to 5 (fully established and active):

Ship Type	Rating (1–5)	Notes
Mentorship		
Allyship		
Sponsorship		
Partnership		
Advocates		
Peer Relationships		
Accountability		
Growth Stretchers		

Step 2: Reflection Questions
- Which ships feel the strongest right now?
- Which ones are missing or weak – and how is that showing up in your career?
- Are there any "deadweight" relationships you're holding onto out of guilt or habit?
- Who have you helped grow this year – and who's helped grow you?
- Which ship will you intentionally build or strengthen over the next 60 days?

Step 3: Ship Goals
- Build: (Which ship will you build from scratch?)
- Strengthen: (Which existing ship will you invest more energy into?)
- Release: (Which ship has served its season and can be let go with gratitude?)
- Stretch: (What relationship will help you grow beyond your current level?)

Final Tip:
Put a calendar reminder 30 days from now to revisit this page. Did you move forward or stay docked? No shame – just strategy.

Because the goal isn't to collect ships.
It's to sail with purpose.

Reflection Recap

Your ships are only as strong as your reflection and action.

Use these prompts to revisit your insights, refine your approach, and realign with your career goals. Don't just read this book – work this book.

Chapter 1: The Mentorship Mirage
- Who are your current mentors, and what role do they play in your career?
- Have you been mistaking access for progress?
- What kind of mentorship are you truly missing – skill-based, situational, or strategic?
- Have you over-indexed on mentorship when you need something more?
- What's one conversation you need to initiate with a mentor to clarify expectations or goals?

Chapter 2: The Allyship Advantage

- Who has advocated for you when you weren't in the room?
- When have you served as an ally to someone else?
- Where in your workplace could allyship be strengthened – and how can you lead that shift?
- Do you show up as your full self at work – and do others feel safe doing the same around you?
- What kind of ally do you want to be known as?

Chapter 3: The Sponsorship Shift

- Do you have someone who is actively opening doors for you?
- What relationships could be nurtured into sponsorship?
- Are you performing at a level that invites sponsorship?
- What are you doing that makes it easy (or hard) for someone to advocate for you?

- How can you start adding value to someone who has influence – without being transactional?

Chapter 4: The Partnership Principle
- Who are your true professional partners – not just collaborators?
- What are the qualities you bring to a strong partnership?
- Are there any partnerships you need to end – or realign?
- How can you deepen a current relationship to become more of a partnership?
- What does an ideal partnership look like for your next level?

Chapter 5: Maintaining the Fleet
- Are you nurturing your current ships – or coasting?
- What systems or habits do you have to stay connected and add value?
- Have you taken anyone in your fleet for granted?
- Who have you thanked recently – sincerely and specifically?

- What one thing can you do this month to maintain or re-engage your career fleet?

Chapter 6: Evolving Your Fleet for Long-Term Success

- What relationships helped me get to this stage of my career?
- Which ones are still aligned with where I'm headed?
- Where do I need to deepen – or release – a connection?
- Who do I admire but haven't reached out to yet?
- What's one way I can evolve my network over the next 90 days?

Final Thought:
Don't rush through these questions. Sit with them. Write about them. Revisit them. Your answers may shift – and that's a sign you're growing.

Because the real career magic?
It happens after the reflection – when you decide to act.

Next Steps / Stay Connected

Your journey doesn't end here – let's keep moving.

Congratulations on making it to the end of *Mind Your 'Ships'*!

If you've made it this far, that means you're serious about building a career that's both strategic and fulfilling.

But don't let this be just another book you highlight and shelf. Let's keep the momentum going:

1. Put Your Reflection Into Action
Go back through your notes, dog-eared pages, and the "Ship Check" Self-Assessment. Pick one ship to focus on over the next 30 days – and set a clear action step. Small, consistent moves create real results.

2. Download Free Tools
Looking for templates, checklists, or bonus videos? Head to www.consultdmcgroup.com/mindyourships for free resources designed to help you deepen what you've learned.

3. Book a Career Strategy Session
Ready to go deeper? Need clarity, confidence, or a game plan to level up? Book a 1:1 career strategy session with Dr. Anesa Davis at www.consultdmcgroup.com. You'll leave with insight, direction, and next steps.

4. Move Now – Don't Stop Here
Loved *Mind Your 'Ships'*? Then you're ready for the next step: the Move Now series. It's a bold, actionable guide to unlocking confidence, influence, and forward momentum in your career.

Whether you're stuck in hesitation, hungry for growth, or ready to show up like you mean it – the *Move Now* book (coming soon!), coaching tools, and digital series are your next power moves.

**Explore more at
www.consultdmcgroup.com/movenow**

5. Let's Connect
LinkedIn: linkedin.com/in/anesadavis
Instagram, Pinterest & TikTok:
@consultdmcgroup
Email: anesa@consultdmcgroup.com

Because this isn't the end – it's just the next move.
Let's build. Let's grow.
And most importantly… let's sail.

About the Author

Dr. Anesa Davis is an award-winning HR executive, speaker, and career strategist who has spent over two decades helping individuals and organizations unlock their potential and create meaningful success.

Known for her bold insights, unapologetic honesty, and contagious energy, Dr. Davis brings a human approach to professional growth. She's built her career inside Fortune 500 companies – advising top executives, leading strategic workforce transformations, and championing diverse talent.

But more than that, she's been in the trenches – navigating office politics, missed opportunities, and the occasional shipwreck of her own.

Through her company, DMC Consulting Group, she empowers professionals to lead with confidence, build strategic relationships, and stop playing small in spaces they've earned. Whether coaching high-potential talent, leading workshops, or writing books like *Mind Your 'Ships*, Dr. Davis is all about equipping people with the mindset and tools to move forward – even when it's scary.

When she's not building empires or helping others build theirs, you can find her traveling, mentoring the next generation of leaders, or reminding folks on LinkedIn that career success isn't about luck – it's about strategy.

Resources

These tools, books, and platforms can support your journey as you build – and mind – your ships.

Recommended Reads
- *The Memo* by Minda Harts
- *Executive Presence* by Sylvia Ann Hewlett
- *The First 90 Days* by Michael Watkins
- *The Sponsor Effect* by Sylvia Ann Hewlett
- *Move Now* by Dr. Anesa Davis (coming soon!)

Career Tools
- CliftonStrengths (gallup.com)
- Predictive Index (predictiveindex.com)
- SHRM Competency Model (shrm.org)
- Career Contessa (careercontessa.com)

Videos & Talks
- TED Talk: 'The Career Advice You Probably Didn't Get' – Susan Colantuono

- TED Talk: 'How to Find Work You Love' – Scott Dinsmore
- LinkedIn Learning: Strategic Networking, Career Management, and Influence Tracks

Templates & Downloads
- Free 'Ship Check' Self-Assessment – www.consultdmcgroup.com/mindyourships
- Networking Message Templates – www.consultdmcgroup.com/resources
- Confidence Tracker & Career Planning Workbook – www.consultdmcgroup.com/resources

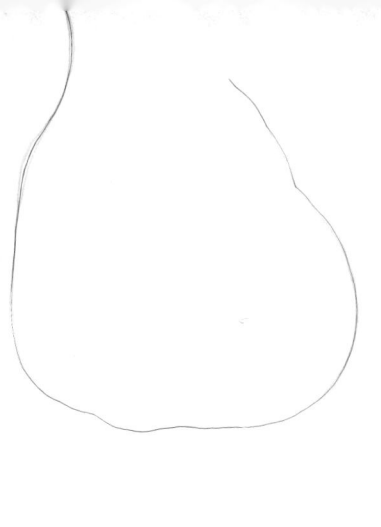

www.ingramcontent.com/pod-product-compliance
Lightning Source LLC
Chambersburg PA
CBHW071146090426
42736CB00012B/2255